This book belongs to:

Name: _____

Date: _____

Contact: _____

_____

Cover art: 'Cedar Waxwing' by Sierra Glassman, 11.
Published in *Stone Soup* Magazine, April, 2018.

Stone Soup, founded in 1973, is published by
Children's Art Foundation—Stone Soup Inc., a
nonprofit organization based in the Unted States.
Find out more at Stonesoup.com.

StoneSoup